P9-BYB-097

GIRLISH

ALANA WULFF

CITADEL PRESS
KENSINGTON PUBLISHING CORP.
www.kensingtonbooks.com

γ٨

CITADEL PRESS BOOKS are published by

Kensington Publishing Corp.
119 West 40th Street
New York, NY 10018

Published by arrangement with Black, Inc. (Australia)

All Kensington titles, imprints, and distributed lines are available at special quantity discounts for bulk purchases for sales promotions, premiums, fund-raising, educational, or institutional use. Special book excerpts or customized printings can also be created to fit specific needs. For details, write or phone the office of the Kensington sales manager: Kensington Publishing Corp., 119 West 40th Street, New York, NY 10018, attn: Sales Department; phone 1-800-221-2647.

ISBN-13: 978-0-8065-3939-3
ISBN-10: 0-8065-3939-9

First Citadel trade paperback printing: August 2019

10 9 8 7 6 5 4 3 2 1

Printed in the United States of America

Electronic edition:

ISBN-13: 978-0-8065-3940-9 (e-book)
ISBN-10: 0-8065-3940-2 (e-book)

Illustrations by Frances Cannon: pp. 11, 63, 85, 147, 169.
Images courtesy of Freepik: pp. 24, 68.

Images courtesy of Shutterstock: africa studio p. 102; anburoshausu p. 178; aPhoenix-Photo pp. 92, 118; Art-Hunters p. 59; ArthurStock p. 113, 155; astarina p. 179; atsurkan p. 117; Azovtsev Maksym p. 70; babayuka p. 39; BeataGFX p. 65; Becky Starsmore p. 151; Brilliantst Studios p. 174; Charcompix pp. 57, 108; CK2 Connect Studio p. 159; designelements p. 163; Diego G Diaz p. 4; Eight Photo p. 90; Evgeny Karandaev p. 72; Evil Pixels Photography p. 144; fascinadora p. 104; Frannyanne p. 86; Greenety p. 97; GooseFrol p. 105; happydancing pp. 54, 102; Heidi Besen p. 43 (top, left); I am Kulz pp. 130, 183; iliveinoctober 166; ikkker p. 67; indigolotos p. 162; inxti p. 88; Jenpol Sumatchaya p. 83; Jiri Hera pp. 71, 140; Karen Roach p. 152; Katya Havok pp. 93, 106; Kostikova Natalia p. 143; Kris Tan p. 173; ksusha27 pp. 79, 146; life morning p. 190; Litho Scratch p. 157; Litvin Diana p. 29; Lunatictm p. 129; Iuri stepanov p. 128; Mallmo pp. 74, 192; Maksim Striganov p. 175; Maxx Satori p. 15; Nadezda Barkova p. 145; nadytok p. 160; NataLT p. 127; Natannee.P, p. 191; Number1411 p. 33; pro-stockstudio p. 168; rawpixel.com p. 95, 140; Ricky LK p. 184; Robert Eastman p. 42; Roman Sotola p. 110; Ryumin Maksim p. 136; SAQUIZETA p. 61; Shannon West p. 43 (bottom); Simikov p. 44, 156; slim p. 177; StockStudio p. 115; surachet khamsuk pp. 13, 23, 60 (blue glitter), 77, 107, 109, 123, 150; TANAKORN TOTABTHAI pp. 46, 60 (gold glitter), 178; Tasiania p. 21, 26, 28, 30; Tendo p. 120; Thankes.Op p. 125; timquo pp. 187, 188; tomertu pp. 35, 180; VADISH ZAINER p. 101; vanilla22 p. 170; Wayne0216 p. 91; Yamabika, p. 99; yul38885 pp. 100, 185. Yurta pp. 146, 181.

Images courtesy of Stocksy: STOCKVANSAR p. 94; Good Vibrations Images p. 111; Tais Ramos Varela p. 149; Wendy Laurel p. 185.

Image courtesy of Unsplash / Laura Ockel p. 47.

THIS BOOK BELONGS TO:

....

THIS YEAR I'M CELEBRATING MY .... BIRTHDAY.

I LOVE BEING ME BECAUSE: ....

....

....

SOMETIMES IT SUCKS BEING A GIRL WHEN: ....

....

THE LAST COMPLIMENT I RECEIVED WAS: ....

....

THE LAST COMPLIMENT I GAVE WAS: ....

....

WHAT MATTERS TO ME MOST IS: ....

....

MY LIFE MOTTO IS: ....

....

....

I'M GOING TO MAKE A DIFFERENCE BY: ....

....

....

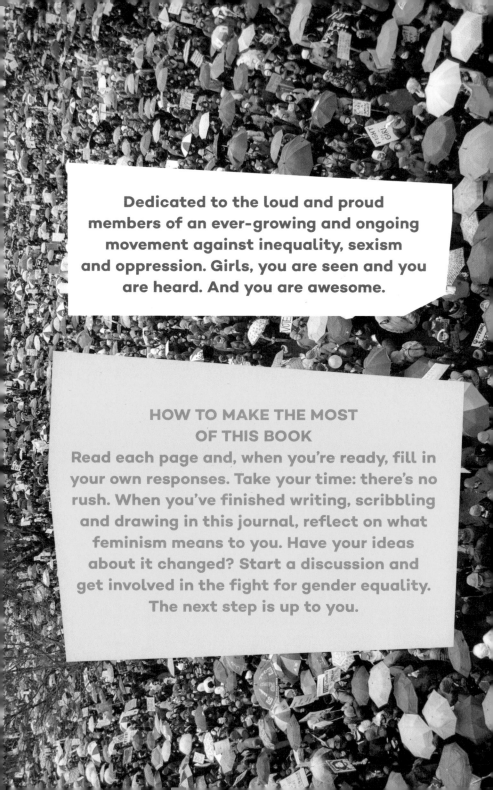

Dedicated to the loud and proud members of an ever-growing and ongoing movement against inequality, sexism and oppression. Girls, you are seen and you are heard. And you are awesome.

HOW TO MAKE THE MOST OF THIS BOOK
Read each page and, when you're ready, fill in your own responses. Take your time: there's no rush. When you've finished writing, scribbling and drawing in this journal, reflect on what feminism means to you. Have your ideas about it changed? Start a discussion and get involved in the fight for gender equality. The next step is up to you.

"A feminist is a person who believes in the power of women just as much as they believe in the power of anyone else. It's equality, it's fairness, and I think it's a great thing to be a part of."

Zendaya

Zendaya is a super talented singer, actor and dancer.
She's also a major fighter for equality and isn't afraid to have her voice heard.

Cool fact? In 2017 Zendaya offered a modeling contract to a young girl who'd been body-shamed on Twitter.

Being a girl freakin' rocks!

We come in all shapes and sizes and from many different walks of life. But no matter what sets us apart, there's one thing that all girls have in common: the right to equality.

Throughout history, women of all ages, races and religions have fiercely battled against inequality and discrimination. They gave their blood, sweat and tears for the rights of women to vote, work, own land, run companies and do what we want with our bodies. For the right to make our own choices about our lives.

Getting to where we are today hasn't been easy, and the battle continues for millions of women across the globe. Despite how far we've come, we're still fighting for the same opportunities as men. We're still campaigning to ensure our voices are heard. And that's not OK. Luckily, young women today care just as much about change as earlier generations, which is why it's now up to us to keep going — to make things better for ourselves, our friends, our families and the girls of the future. I hope this book will light a fire in your belly. Truth be told, that fire is probably already there. If you've ever been treated differently because you're a girl, faced gender discrimination on social media or IRL, or been ignored because you have lady bits, you'll relate to most of what this book is talking about. Or maybe you haven't had those experiences yourself but you've seen them happen to others. Maybe you're sick of it and have been for a while.

"

I want to date,
and shop,
and hang out,
and save the world
from unspeakable demons.
You know...
girly stuff.

—Buffy

"

THE GOAL OF FEMINISM ISN'T TO TAKE AWAY MEN'S RIGHTS, BUT TO IMPROVE THE RIGHTS OF WOMEN.

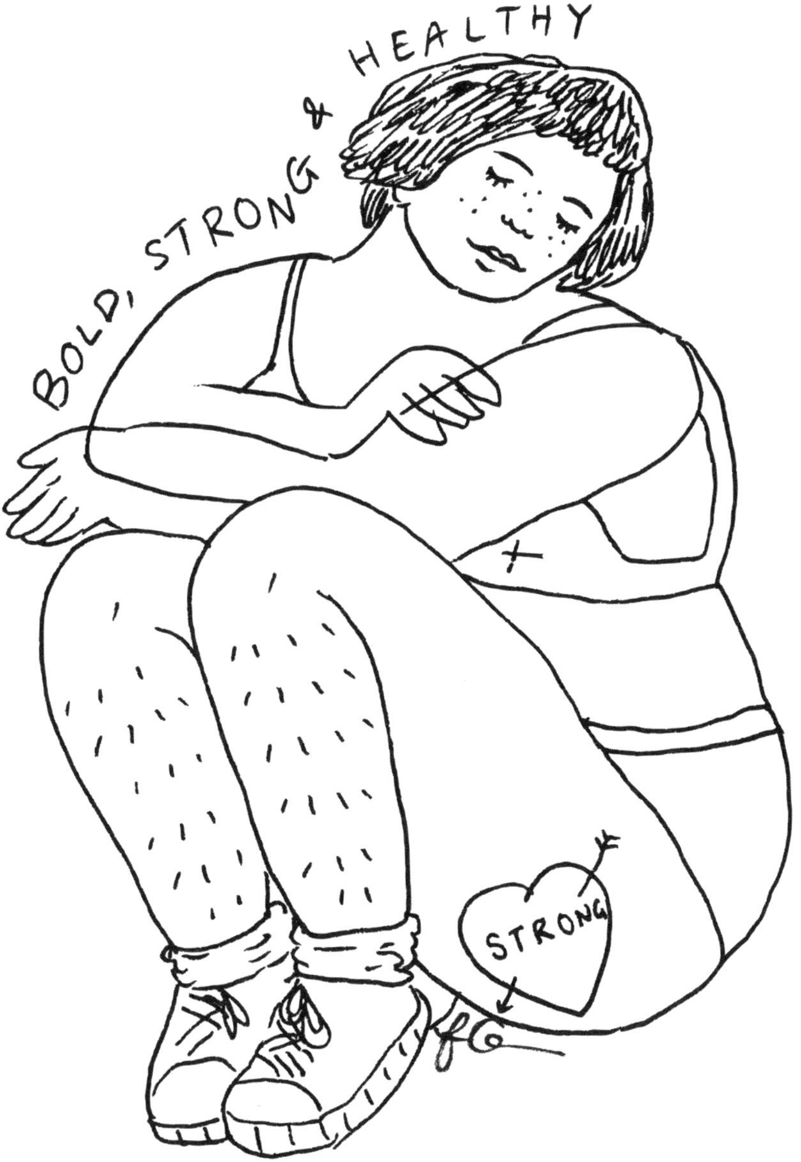
BOLD, STRONG & HEALTHY
STRONG

Why is everyone talking about feminism anyway?

Some girls think that calling yourself a feminist means you have to grow armpit hair, never wear makeup, burn your bra, and hate all men. Unfortunately, there are still HEAPS of people who don't understand that without feminism women wouldn't have the right to vote, pursue our dream jobs, or make decisions about our own bodies.

Feminism is nothing to be scared of. This movement for equality has the power to change lives, to change the future of girls and women throughout the world. As feminists, we are fighting on behalf of ALL women. Because honestly, how can we truly succeed when others are being held back? While feminism addresses the inequality between women and men, it's also a very broad movement that goes beyond this. It doesn't just include girls and women from middle-class backgrounds in first-world countries. It includes women of color, trans women, queer women, LGBTQI+ women, those who identify as non-binary as well as those who are cisgender, and anyone who has been disadvantaged or pushed down by the patriarchy. As activist and author Gloria Steinem once said, "A feminist is anyone who recognizes the equality and full humanity of women and men." Now … what the heck is wrong with that?

52% OF THE WORLD'S POPULATION IS FEMALE.

"Some people ask, 'Why the word feminist? Why not just say you are a believer in human rights, or something like that?' Because that would be dishonest. Feminism is, of course, part of human rights in general – but to choose to use the vague expression human rights is to deny the specific and particular problem of gender."

Chimamanda Ngozi Adichie

Adichie is a Nigerian author who has published three novels, as well as short stories and non-fiction. Adichie turned her hugely popular 2012 TedX talk "We Should All Be Feminists" into a book-length essay of the same name. Fun fact? Audio from the actual speech was included in Beyoncé's 2013 hit "Flawless".

Circle the sentences that speak to you the most.

I am new to feminism but can't wait to learn.

I know a bit about feminism
but I need to know more.

I am a feminist expert
and want to encourage other girls
to join the ranks.

I am sick of being treated
differently from boys.

I need some inspiration to go out
and make a difference.

I'm SO OVER not being taken seriously.

I'm tired of feeling unsafe.

I want to help give all girls a voice.

I don't believe in oppression
or inequality.

I am the future and real change
starts with me.

"Feminism is not a rule book, but a discussion. A conversation. A process."

Tavi Gevinson

After hitting it big in the blogosphere at the age of 12 with *Style Rookie*, Tavi Gevinson went on to become the founder and editor-in-chief of *Rookie* — a website for all things teen, including pop culture, feminism, lifestyle and wellness. Tavi's been so successful she's appeared in the famous Forbes "30 under 30" list and is now transitioning into acting.

WOMEN'S RIGHTS ARE HUMAN RIGHTS

Write down the first five words that come to mind when you think of the word "feminism" – don't overthink it, just write!

1

2

3

4

5

Now ask other women around you – your mom, aunts, neighbors and friends – the same question. What words did they come up with? Were they the same as yours? Why not ask your dad or brother as well? By chatting about feminism with the people in your life, you're starting a super important conversation.

Way back in 1776 when John Adams was writing the US Constitution, his wife Abigail Adams warned him not to forget women:

"If particular care and attention is not paid to the ladies, we are determined to foment a rebellion, and will not hold ourselves bound by any laws in which we have no voice or representation."

Whaddya know? John didn't listen. Can't say we didn't give a heads up…

Know Your Herstory

... Yep, that was a feminist pun!

Long before we had Insta, Tumblr, Snapchat and camera phones ready to capture and broadcast every moment of our lives, there were protests, marches and battles being fought to ensure the next generation of girls weren't going to have to suffer in a male-dominated world. These historical movements changed the course of women's rights forever. Perhaps you already know a lot about feminist history – but if it's new to you, or you want a refresher, here's a quick rundown ...

While there have been feminists for as long as there have been females, feminism is usually spoken about in three movements, or waves (not forgetting all the mini movements we participate in each day when we stand up to gender bias and fight the system – #yass). These three waves were mainly about what was going on in the Western world – the UK, US, Canada and Australia in particular – but that's not all the ladies out there, is it?

The first wave

To get super basic — back in the late 19th and early 20th centuries, women weren't allowed to vote or own property in their own name, and higher education was just for dudes. Men spoke for women and owned everything. The ladies behind this first wave — who were sometimes called suffragettes — knew they had to get political, and fought for the right to vote.

Around 1848, Elizabeth Cady Stanton and a group of powerful women gathered at the Seneca Falls Convention in New York and created the Declaration of Sentiments and Resolutions. This declaration was filled to the brim with all the #goals for their very own women's movement. Fast-forward almost 70 years (yep, that long) and women were finally granted the right to vote in the United States in 1920.

"It's time we break through taboos and start opening conversations within our communities."

— Mariah Idrissi

Mariah is a young British speaker and activist. She was also H&M's first hijab-wearing model back in 2015.

NEW ZEALAND WAS THE FIRST COUNTRY TO GIVE WOMEN THE RIGHT TO VOTE, IN 1893. WOMEN IN SAUDI ARABIA WERE ONLY GRANTED THE RIGHT TO VOTE IN 2015.

YOUR VOICE

Even though you might not be old enough to vote yet, you know how good it feels when your opinions are heard and valued, right? And you probably also know how crappy it feels to be ignored or when decisions are made for you.

Can you recall a time when you weren't listened to because you are a girl? How did you respond? What would you do differently next time?

"You don't make progress by standing on the sidelines, whimpering and complaining. You make progress by implementing ideas."

Shirley Chisholm

In 1968, Shirley Chisholm became the first black woman elected to the United States Congress.

The second wave

Liberation! Say it with me! Second-wave feminism is possibly the most well-known wave of the three — mainly because we've been bombarded with the idea that women were burning their bras and braiding their leg hair at the time ... And some of them probably were. Good for them! OK, truth? The bra-burning was a bit of a myth. But during the '60s and '70s, activists and authors like Gloria Steinem, Betty Friedan, Dorothy Pitman Hughes and Maya Angelou helped women discover their true selves. They helped liberate women from the kitchen. Second-wave feminism was born out of the notion that women were not just maids — not just Suzy Homemaker—types eagerly waiting for their husbands to return home after a long day at work, with a drink in one hand and dinner on the table. The issues that second-wave feminism fought over were legal and social, and included things like sex discrimination, the pay gap, reproductive rights, representation in the government, awareness of violence against women, and our roles outside the home.

While second-wave feminists made huge progress, some reckon that the movement fell apart because of internal divisions. Instead of fighting together as one — black, white, straight, gay, who had more money (or "privilege") — feminists started fighting each other. What a waste of good talent and effort!

"Economic equity is an enormous empowerment of women. Having jobs that provide income means that women can be a more effective force, a more equal force, in the political process. Women with income take themselves more seriously and they are taken more seriously."

Betty Friedan

Betty Friedan wrote the incredible book *The Feminist Mystique*, which challenged the convention of the woman's place being in the home and is often credited with starting the second wave of feminism. In 1964 her book sold over one million copies.

The third wave

The 1980s and '90s were a funny old time for feminism. Some of the women who should have considered themselves feminists (the ones who now had all the rights the other feminists fought so hard for) suddenly didn't want to be called "feminist". There was a whole bunch of women who didn't like the protesting, armpit-hair-growing, angry ways of the '60s and '70s, and thought this was the only way to be a feminist. They wanted to wear makeup and high heels, and have big hair — hey, guess what, ladies? You can wear lipstick and still be a feminist!

Third-wave feminists — those women still eager to fight — took different feminist theories and placed them smack bang on the table for everyone to see. The daughters of the second-wave feminists wanted to do it their own way, and redefined what it was to be a feminist by including women from all backgrounds, races, religions, socioeconomic standings and more. The biggest change in this part of herstory is that feminism went from being a movement to being more of a solo sport. Sisters were doing it for themselves, and sometimes doing it by themselves. It was a time when the world tried to convince us that because we had the vote and we were allowed to work, the need for feminism was over. Ah, sorry guys, you couldn't have been more wrong.

Pizza not patriarchy!

Fourth wave?

Hey, so this is the part where you come in. And it's up to you to make your contribution count. The key message from this majorly woke generation is FEMINISM IS FOR EVERYONE. Inclusion is the key. To make a real difference, feminism should be accessible to everyone — it's as simple as that. That's why the power of this movement doesn't just lie in the numbers or the history; it lies in the kickass, unique women from all across the world who call themselves feminists. The Women's March of 2017 was just one excellent example of what can happen when all women support each other and fight the same fight. It was the largest one-day demonstration in political history, and we made it happen! And you guys have something that no other generation before you had. Yep, the power of social media. It's almost like a throwback to the second-wave feminists' mass protests, except so much better, because you can be heard on your own terms, connect with anyone in the world, and do it from anywhere. Oh, and you know what else you have? BEYONCÉ. Boom — mic drop.

#thefutureisfemale

"I feel like we should stop calling feminists 'feminists' and just start calling people who aren't feminist 'sexist' – and then everyone else is just a human. You are either a normal person or a sexist."

Maisie Williams

Maisie Williams is best known for her role as the kickass, independent and seriously capable Arya Stark in the television series *Game of Thrones*.

PROTECT
TRANS KIDS
PROTECT
YOUNG GIRLS
PROTECT
OLDER WOMEN
PROTECT
QUEER TEENS
PROTECT
GIRLS OF COLOR
PROTECT
EACH OTHER

"When you are a marginalized person or a woman of color and/or someone who's a part of the LGBTQI+ community, your acts become politicized, just by being yourself."

Amandla Stenberg

Amandla Stenberg is a famous actress and celebrated activist. She made headlines when she came out as bisexual on *Teen Vogue*'s Snapchat in 2016.

If you're not fighting for all women, you're fighting for no women.

"I am a proud black feminist and womanist, and I'm extremely proud of the work that's being done. I'm a feminist who wants not only to hear the term intersectionality but actually feel it, and see the evolution of what intersectional feminism can actually achieve. I want women's rights to be equally honored, and uplifted, and heard ... but I want to see us fighting the fight for all women – women of color, our LGBTQ sisters, our Muslim sisters. I want to see millions of us marching out there for our rights, and I want to see us out there marching for the rights of women like Dajerria Becton, who was body-slammed by a cop while she was in her swimsuit for simply existing as a young, vocal black girl. I think we are inching closer and closer there, and for that, I am very proud."

Solange

Singer, songwriter, model, and actress – is there anything this girl can't do? Sister to mega star Beyoncé, Solange Knowles is an advocate for feminism and racial equality. Her revolutionary album, "A Seat at the Table" was one of the most culturally significant music releases in recent times and tackled everything from empowerment to cultural appropriation and racism.

WOMEN TO KNOW ABOUT

Here's a list of loud and proud feminists who have made a difference – how many have you heard of? Circle the ones you know and research the ones you don't. Who else would you add to this list?

Mary Wollstonecraft

Elizabeth Cady Stanton

Emmeline Pankhurst

Elizabeth Blackwell

Sojourner Truth

Simone de Beauvoir

Eleanor Roosevelt

Marlene Dietrich

Coco Chanel

Betty Friedan

Gloria Steinem

bell hooks

Coretta Scott King

Maya Angelou

Alice Walker

Hillary Clinton

Oprah Winfrey

Ruth Bader Ginsburg

Madonna

Tegla Loroupe

Sheryl Sandberg

Malala Yousafzai

Chimamanda Ngozi Adichie

Beyoncé

Emma Watson

Tavi Gevinson

Rowan Blanchard

Amandla Stenberg

What are the moments in feminist history
that you wish you could have been
a part of and why?

BE A GIRL ON A MISSION

> "Women, if the soul of the nation is to be saved, I believe that you must become its soul."

Coretta Scott King

When Coretta Scott King first uttered this mighty statement in 1970, who knew it would still hold so much power and relevance today? Coretta wasn't just the wife of Martin Luther King Jr – she was an author, civil rights leader, and activist in her own right. Coretta knew how important women were to activism and took this knowledge to help lead the Civil Rights Movement. She encouraged girls from all generations to have their voices heard.

The personal is political

Every revolution starts with an idea and an action. What are some of the things you can do to start your own feminist revolution? This doesn't have to be a massive feat or an overwhelming idea. It might be affirmations that you tell yourself each day or chatting to your teacher about encouraging a more inclusive environment, or reading one more book a month. Start small and then go big.

1. _____

   _____

2. _____

   _____

3. _____

   _____

4. _____

   _____

5. _____

   _____

Imagine you're heading to a women's rights march.
Draw your protest sign. What does it look like?
Does it use a symbol? Powerful words?
A personal message? What does it say about you?

Looking to make a difference locally
but not sure where to start? Take it to the
top! Find the contact details of your local
representatives or council members
and get in touch about the women's issues
that concern you and other girls
in your community.

"Don't be a fool, there is no such thing as just a girl."

Elissa Schappell

Elissa Schappell is an American writer. Her short story collection *Blueprints for Building Better Girls* is actually the best thing ever.

Girls don't want boys.

Girls want

equal pay

and

rad tunes.

LANGUAGE MATTERS

It's not news that gender inequality starts early in life. Why is "running like a girl" a bad thing, and why are boys urged to "be a man" like that's a good thing? Why do little boys get told they're clever and little girls get told they're pretty?

Hidden meanings in everyday phrases create involuntary bias, and excuse the actions of boys while at the same time placing blame on girls. Phrases such as "boys will be boys," "it takes two to tango" and "he's picking on you because he likes you" send the message that girls shouldn't be offended by unwanted attention from boys and boys don't have to stop doing it. It's the beginning of a blame game that always sees girls getting the short end of the stick.

Why is this so important, you may ask? Because language has influenced the way women have been perceived, treated and valued in the world since the beginning of time. By using language that unites us and doesn't divide us — or language that doesn't gender people — we're giving everyone the same opportunities to have their voices heard and feel respected. The way we talk about girls, the way we talk about their success, and also their future ambition relies on a language system that treats everyone equally.

"I'm not bossy.
I'm the boss."

Beyoncé

Queen Bey was once described by a critic in
the *New Yorker* as "the most important and
compelling popular musician of the twenty-first
century".

SHE HEARS ...	SHE THINKS ...
"She's such a bossy boots."	"I shouldn't be assertive."
"She's a feisty one."	"I shouldn't give my opinion." "I shouldn't stand up for myself."
"Why are you being so uptight?"	"I shouldn't have boundaries."
"She can be a real know-it-all."	"I shouldn't say things that make me sound clever."
"She's a bit of a tomboy."	"I shouldn't be myself." "I shouldn't play the sports that I like." "I should look more feminine." "I shouldn't dress the way I like." "I am judged on my appearance."
"She's a little princess."	"I shouldn't be myself." "I should look less feminine." "I shouldn't dress the way I like." "I am judged on my appearance."

From the Australian government's 'Excuse Interpreter', which
decodes misogynistic and damaging language that's often used as
justification in abuse of women.

"No" is a complete sentence

"I just love bossy women. I could be around them all day. To me, bossy isn't a pejorative term at all. It means somebody's passionate and engaged and ambitious and doesn't mind leading."

Amy Poehler

Amy might just be one of the funniest women on the planet. She's an actress, comedian, director, producer and writer. Not only did she play the "cool mom" in *Mean Girls* and Leslie Knope in *Parks and Recreation*, she's also been besties with Tina Fey since they first started out on the comedy scene together. Amy is extra amazing because she also runs an organization called, "Smart Girls," which is dedicated to helping young adults become their authentic selves by emphasizing brains and creativity over "fitting in."

If you're not a fan of being called nasty names or gross words, don't call anyone else those things either.

"If there's one thing you'd never catch me doing it's commenting on someone's appearance, sexuality or race in that way."

Lorde

Lorde's real name is Ella Marija Lani Yelich-O'Connor and she was born in New Zealand in 1996. You know the rest.

Sometimes words are used to hurt or bring us down. Here are some words and phrases associated with being female that have negative connotations.

Bossy
Princess
Bitchy
High maintenance
Emotional
Feisty

Know it all
Just a girl
Irrational
Opinionated
Hysterical
Run like a girl

Can you think of others?

Facepalm: Mansplaining

We've all been there — it's that really annoying moment when a guy tries to explain or tell you about something you already know — as if he's doing you a favor and helping you learn about the world ... Ugh. The Merriam-Webster dictionary defines mansplaining as "when a man talks condescendingly to someone (especially a woman) about something he has incomplete knowledge of, with the mistaken assumption that he knows more about it than the person he's talking to does."

The next time a dude gets on his high horse around you, you could bust out one of these one-liners:

1. "There's no need to explain."
2. "You can stop interrupting me now."
3. "Why don't I explain it to you?"
4. "Yep, I literally just said that."
5. "Unless I ask, I don't need you to explain anything to me."

Of course, you could also utter the best line from *Mean Girls*: "You can go shave your back now."

What other nifty one-liners could you use against mansplainers?

....

....

....

Create a list of feel-good and encouraging words you would like to use more often. Stuck for ideas? Think about the way you'd describe your best friend or someone you admire.

GUIDELINES FOR RESPECT:

TREAT YOURSELF WITH KINDNESS

SUPPORT YOUR FELLOW WOMEN

BELIEVE YOU CAN DO WHATEVER
YOU PUT YOUR MIND TO

DRESS THE WAY YOU WANT

STAND UP FOR YOURSELF

SPEAK YOUR MIND

ENCOURAGE OTHERS

BE A VOICE FOR CHANGE

DON'T SETTLE FOR INEQUALITY

VOICE YOUR OPINIONS IN PUBLIC
AND IN PRIVATE

BE SEEN AND HEARD

WOMEN TO WHOA ABOUT

Mary Sherman Morgan

Oh, hey there, rocket girl! Mary Sherman Morgan was America's first female rocket scientist and the inventor of the liquid fuel, Hydyne, which powered the rocket that shot America's very first satellite, Explorer 1, into orbit.

Working alongside 900 male scientists at North American Aviation back in the 1950s, Mary was one of the many unsung female heroes of the space age whose impact on space exploration wasn't truly recognized or acknowledged until recently. #reachingskyhigh

BEING FAMOUS ON INSTA IS LIKE BEING RICH IN MONOPOLY

KEYBOARD ACTIVISM

Social media has huge potential for raising awareness about feminism.

Based on data from Twitter, discussions around feminism have increased by 300% on their platform in the last three years.

Beyoncé's VMA performance with the word "feminist" on stage resulted in a 64% increase in feminist conversations on Twitter, while Emma Watson's #HeForShe speech led to almost twice as many tweets using the word "feminism."

Like for love

The online space is a mixed bag. One minute we're being lifted up by a community of supporters, confidantes and allies, and the next we're fending off trolls and bullies. Having a presence and an opinion online (as many of us do these days) gives us the opportunity to express ourselves, raise awareness for campaigns we are passionate about and connect to like-minded individuals from around the world. But it also opens us up to threats, sexism, racism, slut-shaming, fat-shaming and so much more. This is especially sh*t considering how much time the average teen spends online: nine hours a day. Is it any wonder that the rates of depression and anxiety are rising?

While connecting to others online can create a self-esteem boost when things go well, social media can also encourage us to compare ourselves to others and expose us to online bullying. The result is unrealistic body images, pressure, fear of missing out, self-esteem issues and disconnection from what really matters in life.

HIM: If you really liked me, you'd send me a sexy pic.

ME: If you really respected me, you wouldn't ask me to.

Cheese and bacon rolls, not online trolls.

"Use your heartache as motivation for the future. When I was cyberbullied, it definitely ruined my life for a period of time and I just kept turning the other cheek and knowing that if I worked hard at my dreams, that one day they will have no choice but to hear me and see my face everywhere they went and one day they will say 'I knew that girl in school' rather than 'I bullied this girl.' Don't give them what you want, keep fighting and keep pushing cause you never know where you'll be there one day."

Demi Lovato

Superstar Demi might be known for her mad singing and acting skills, but it's her self-love beliefs and anti-bullying efforts that are creating headlines these days.

Online

— vs —

IRL

Do you behave differently online
from how you behave IRL?

How is your online identity different?

Have you ever felt pressure to create a
different version of "you" to show to the world?

The internet's not all bad, right?
Who are your fave voices online?
Who can't you get enough of?

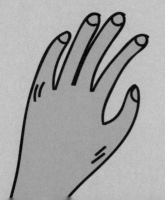

NO
CONNECTION_

While many of us are growing up in a 24/7 digital world, it's easy to forget that not all teens have access to technology. This means that certain teens end up being excluded from education opportunities and potential future employment, as well as interaction with other kids their age. Many women in developing countries face this issue: for political, economical and technological reasons, they don't have access to the internet. Without victimizing these individuals, we need to do our bit to help their voices be heard. We can do this by inspiring other girls to use social media in order to spread important messages around equality, making sure our online activism doesn't entirely replace our IRL activism, and continuing to talk about gender inequality. The more we speak up, the harder it is to ignore us. Let's use social media for good, not evil.

From Hermione Granger to Princess leia, Starr Carter to Katniss Everdeen, some of the best characters ever created have been female — women who are strong, independent, funny, smart and here to tell their story. But whatever you think about gender equality in Hollywood and the greater pop culture universe, it's safe to say it's been a long road from damsel in distress to leading lady. Tbh, it's been exhausting. And while the roles for all women are slowly starting to diversify, it's only because we've ensured that our roles as women in the real world have morphed and developed along the way as well. Movies, television and entertainment have a major influence on society, and the link between what's happening out there in the world and what we're seeing on screen, on stage, on the catwalk or on the page shouldn't be ignored. That's why it's so important to keep fighting for equality IRL — so that it translates across all the mediums that we consume every day.

Think about your favorite movies, television shows and web series. What can you say about the female characters on screen? Are they all represented the same way? Is there enough diversity in what you're watching or would you like to see more? Which characters do you connect to and why?

WOMEN TO WHOA ABOUT

LaDonna Brave Bull Allard

When the Dallas-based Energy Transfer Partners (ETP) made the decision to redirect a portion of an oil pipeline underneath the Missouri River to the top of Lake Oahe in North Dakota in 2016, activist, historian and genealogist for the Standing Rock Sioux Tribe, LaDonna Brave Bull Allard, took a stand.

LaDonna recognized the gross violation of indigenous peoples' rights, as well as the risk to the preservation of the historic site and the water supply. She went on to set up resistance camps at the Dakota Access Pipeline, and was joined by thousands of activists from tribes around the country. Together they fought the establishment — even when there were attempts to subdue and restrain protestors with tear gas, fire hoses, and rubber bullets.

A girl with an education is unstoppable

"Nowhere on earth do women have as many opportunities as men. Nowhere. But in every single way, life is much harder for girls and women in the poorest countries compared with both their female counterparts in the developed world and their male counterparts in the developing world."

girlscount.one.org

#girlscount

TRUTH BOMB

130 MILLION GIRLS ACROSS THE WORLD DON'T HAVE ACCESS TO EDUCATION.

Sure, homework can suck, but education changes lives when it breaks the poverty cycle and ensures girls are less likely to marry early or against their will. When girls and women receive an education, they're less vulnerable to disease, less likely to marry young and experience severe complications during childbirth, and more likely to have healthy babies and eventually send these children to school.

"

One child,
one teacher, one book
and one pen can
change the world.
Education is the
only solution.
Education first.

—Malala Yousafzai

"

The girl fighting back

Malala Yousafzai was just 11 years old when she started writing a blog about her passion for the education of girls and her fears that her school in Pakistan would be attacked. Shortly thereafter, in a documentary for the *New York Times*, Malala was revealed as the author behind the blog. When she was 15, as Malala was returning home from school one day, a masked member of the Taliban boarded her school bus, asked for her by name and shot her in the head. Miraculously, Malala survived.

This attempt on her life was reported throughout the world and within weeks, more than 2 million people signed a right to education petition, and the National Assembly ratified Pakistan's first Right to Free and Compulsory Education Bill. Malala continues to fight to raise awareness of the social and economic impact of girls' education.

Malala has since gone on to accept the Nobel Peace Prize, donating her prize money of more than $500,000 to creating a secondary school for girls in Pakistan.

YES
SHE
CAN

"**No matter where you're from, your dreams are valid.**"

Lupita Nyong'o

Lupita Nyong'o is an award-winning actress and a writer, director and producer. In 2016 she launched an anti-poaching campaign through her organization Wildaid.

"The saddest thing a girl can do is dumb herself down for a guy."

Emma Watson

Emma Watson rocked it as Hermione Granger in the Harry Potter series, but did you know she also graduated with a degree in English Literature and is a certified yoga and meditation teacher? Oh, and she's also a United Nations Goodwill Ambassador who was pivotal in launching the super powerful HeForShe campaign.

DON'T BE
AFRAID
TO BE THE
SMARTEST
PERSON
IN THE ROOM

"I never cut class. I loved getting As. I liked being smart. I liked being on time. I thought being smart is cooler than anything in the world."

Michelle Obama

Former First Lady of the USA Michelle Obama is an American lawyer and writer, a role model for women and an advocate for poverty awareness.

Have you ever been scared to put your hand up in class? Did you do it anyway? Did this help you realize there was nothing to freak about? How did the moment make you feel? Did it give you the confidence to speak up at school more?

WOMEN TO WHOA ABOUT

Ruth Bader Ginsburg

They don't call her 'The Notorious RBG' for nothin'.

She's the OG boss lady who's seen it all. Associate Justice of the Supreme Court, Ruth Bader Ginsburg, is one woman you don't want to mess with. With more than 25 years on the bench as the 107th Supreme Court justice, RBG is only one of four women to hold the position and has spent much of her time in power fighting for women's rights, gender equality, and the fair treatment of marginalized groups across America.

Leading the Way

The climb to the top can be tough for anyone, but it's particularly hard for women. Often higher standards are set for women, we're judged by different criteria, and our accomplishments are rewarded differently. But why?

As women, we're taught by society to underestimate our abilities, to not rock the boat, to tiptoe around negotiating our pay, to put up with all kinds of treatment, and to focus on simply having a job instead of advancing in one. Along with a lack of organizations willing to hire women for top positions, this means it's way more doom and gloom for women in leadership roles than it should be.

Some people think women aren't tough enough (puh-lease) or that we don't have enough experience to run countries or lead multibillion-dollar companies. We need to make women in leadership more visible so that young girls throughout the world have the confidence to reach the top. We need to make our voices heard and smash through those boardroom doors and glass ceilings with full force.

"

We have *still*
not shattered that
highest and hardest
glass ceiling,
but someday
someone will.

—Hillary Clinton

"

These are just a handful of countries that have experienced a woman in power:

AUSTRALIA
GERMANY
ARGENTINA
BANGLADESH
LITHUANIA
BRAZIL
KOSOVO
DENMARK
SOUTH KOREA
SENEGAL
NORWAY
LATVIA
CHILE
MALTA
SWITZERLAND
POLAND
CROATIA
SLOVENIA
TAIWAN
NEW ZEALAND

COMMUNITY LEADERSHIP

Raising the status of girls and women in leadership positions within small and rural communities has a huge effect on education and the economy. It even has health and social benefits for everyone – not just women! In Aboriginal communities, women are often the influencers, decision-makers and initiators of projects that improve the lives of many families in their local areas. Statistically, Aboriginal women are more likely to finish high school and are therefore more likely than Aboriginal men to take on leadership roles.

AMPLIFY!

Did you know that during Barack Obama's presidency, the women in his staff created their own strategy to make sure they weren't ignored or overlooked? Pretty cool, huh? They knew it was going to be super hard to crack the code of a male-dominated administration, so these clever gals started using amplification to ensure their ideas were being recognized. What does this mean exactly? It means that whenever a woman was overlooked or interrupted by a man, the other women in the room repeated the ignored idea until it was properly heard and considered. This forced the guys in the room to listen up and take notice! During a chat with the *Washington Post*, former White House senior adviser Valerie Jarrett explained that the strategy certainly paid off. "It's fair to say that there was a lot of testosterone flowing in those early days. Now we have a little more estrogen that provides a counterbalance." Hey, you gotta start somewhere!

"I love to see a young girl go out and grab the world by the lapels. Life's a b*tch. You've got to go out and kick ass."

Maya Angelou

Maya Angelou was a writer, novelist and civil rights activist. She wrote some of the most famous books in the world. Her memoir *I Know Why the Caged Bird Sings* made literary history as the first nonfiction bestseller by an African-American woman.

Who runs the World?

GIRLS!

"We are speaking up for those who don't have anyone listening to them, for those who can't talk about it just yet, and for those who will never speak again."

EMMA GONZÁLEZ

This Parkland school shooting survivor isn't just a changemaker or activist – she's a fierce female advocate for gun control and has already changed US history. González quickly became the face of the March for Our Lives campaign and helped organize the globally recognized protest in less than ten days

SHEROES
NOT
HEROES

Be the kind of leader you'd want to follow.

LIST THE QUALITIES YOU THINK MAKE A GREAT LEADER:

....

....

....

....

....

....

....

....

....

....

Now circle the qualities that are traditionally thought of as male. Are any of these qualities traditionally thought of as female? What's wrong with that picture?

Have you ever wanted to run for class or school president? If so, what would you campaign for? What are the issues that matter to you?

Sometimes the way we believe
in ourselves and other girls can get mixed up
without us realizing. Have you ever caught
yourself secretly thinking that boys are
better at certain things than girls?
Jot down your feelings below.

Who are the female leaders you admire the most?

_____

_____

_____

_____

_____

_____

_____

_____

_____

_____

_____

OH. MY. GODDESS.

TWO OF THE HIGHEST IQ SCORES EVER RECORDED BELONG TO WOMEN.

"It is better to look ahead and prepare than look back and regret."

JACQUELINE JOYNER-KERSEE

Jacqueline Joyner-Kersee is one of the greatest Olympic athletes the US has ever seen and continues to inspire girls across the country each and every day.

"Jackie," as she's often referred to, won three gold, one silver and two bronze Olympic medals during her competitive career. She was also the first woman to ever score more than 7,000 points in the heptathlon event at the 1986 Goodwill Games. Just two years later at the 1988 Summer Olympics, she became the first American woman to win gold in the long jump AND gold in the heptathlon.

#aimhigh #jumphigher

Since retiring, Jackie has used her public platform to support women's rights, education, and racial equality. Oh, and she's still the most awarded female track and field Olympian in history. No biggie.

EVEN THOUGH THE ANCIENT GREEKS HELD THE HERAEAN GAMES (THE FIRST WOMEN'S ATHLETIC COMPETITION) AS EARLY AS THE 6TH CENTURY BC, WOMEN WEREN'T ALLOWED TO COMPETE IN THE OLYMPICS UNTIL 1900!

RUN
LIKE A GIRL

THROW
LIKE A GIRL

FIGHT
LIKE A GIRL

In 1962, at just 20 years of age, Kathrine Switzer was the first woman to ever officially register and run the Boston Marathon in the United States. After registering as "K.V. Switzer", Kathrine's history-making run was nearly ruined by a male race official named Jock Semple, who tried to physically drag her from the course. Luckily fellow runners intervened – allowing her to finish the race as planned. The photos of the event are still some of the most searched-for images online.

"I'm not the next Usain Bolt or Michael Phelps. I'm the first Simone Biles."

Simone Biles

Simone Biles is the most decorated American gymnast of all time! In 2016 she led the US Olympic women's gymnastics team, nicknamed "The Final Five," to a gold medal.

"Find solidarity, find other people who are having the same struggles or who are maybe a couple of years ahead of you in the process, and talk to them."

Lindy West

Lindy is a US-based writer, feminist and activist. She's all about body positivity, finding your voice, and accepting the beauty of who you are.

strength

recognizes

strength

"Those of us who understand, who feel strongly, must not tire. We must not give up. We must persist."

Wangari Maathai

Wangari Maathai was an internationally renowned and celebrated environmental activist and Nobel laureate from Kenya.

Who are the amazing women in your life?
Are they teachers, grandmothers,
stepmothers, mothers, older sisters or aunts?
What makes them so special and
inspirational?
What are some of the talents and qualities
you admire in them the most?

....

inspires me because she

....

....

inspires me because she

....

....

inspires me because she

....

....

inspires me because she

....

"I think teenage girls are going to save the world! That age group just seems to be holding people accountable. They have a really strong voice – and a loud one."

Katy Perry

She kissed a girl and she liked it, she roared and we heard it – and now Katy Perry is chaining herself to a new rhythm. The famous singer-songwriter once proclaimed she wasn't a feminist, but has since realized the importance of equality. Katy recently got two thumbs up from feminist activist Gloria Steinem, and was also one of the most outspoken Hillary Clinton supporters in the 2016 US presidential election.

Now that you've thought about the women who really matter to you, why not sit down and have a chat with one or all of them? Interview them about their experiences in life as a woman. What was life like for girls when they were your age? How did they see their future? Do they have advice for girls your age?

"I dropped out of school when I was in 11th grade from bullying. That decision saved my life and allowed me to become who I am today, even if at the time my family wasn't the kindest to my mom for pulling me out of school. I went on to get my high school diploma and never looked back. To the weird kids, the fat kids, the kids who's [sic] skin is darker than most, the kids who having learning disabilities, the kids who eat alone at lunch, the kids who are too afraid to live their truth because society has shown you that you don't belong let me say this: YOU MATTER."

Tess Holliday

Tess Holliday is a plus-size supermodel and a dedicated advocate for body positivity and feminism. She's also a mom and a best-selling author, so you know, she's legit crushing this little thing we call life.

Tess doesn't subscribe to fat shaming or online bullying, which is why she created the über popular hashtag #effyourbeautystandards back in 2013.

"The success of every woman should be the inspiration to another. We should raise each other up. Make sure you're very courageous: be strong, be extremely kind, and above all, be humble."

Serena Williams

One of the world's most accomplished athletes, Serena has made a household name for herself as one of the greatest tennis players of all time.

BEING
A
GIRL
IS
YOUR
SUPERPOWER

"Our greatest obligation is to keep reaching, to continue growing, to push beyond what seems possible, to live outside the boxes created for us."

ELAINE WELTEROTH

As the former Editor-In-Chief of *Teen Vogue* (yes, the Bible), Elaine's leadership was so powerful that she legit disrupted the global discourse when she commissioned Lauren Duca's highly acclaimed piece, "Donald Trump is Gaslighting America." The article put the teen publication back on the map and solidified Welteroth's place as an advocate for women and teens across America.

Welteroth went on to expand *Teen Vogue*'s content to include cultural, social and political issues, which gave real-life legends like Amandla Stenberg and Rowan Blanchard the chance to reach more girls with their messages of empowerment and intersectionality.

Cool fact? Earlier in her career, Welteroth was also the first black beauty director in the history of Conde Nast. Go you good thing!

Me and my girls

There's nothing we wouldn't do for our besties. They lend us a shoulder to cry on when the going gets tough, they are our partners in crime when life gets crazy, and they always let us borrow an emergency outfit when we're stuck for something to wear. It's no wonder we classify these hardcore friends as part of our squads, crews, groups or girl gangs.

Girl squads CAN be amazing and positive. But real squad goals should be about empowering each other without disempowering others.

BESTIE BENEFITS

1. There's never a shortage of things to laugh about.

2. You can tell them anything.

3. They never judge you.

4. They always support you.

5. They always understand you.

6. You share in each other's successes.

7. They're your biggest fans.

8. They always make time for you.

9. They make the ordinary extraordinary.

10. They'll always tell you the truth.

What do your best friends mean to you? Why not write them a thank-you letter for always being there when you need them? What are some of the funniest moments you've been through, or the toughest challenges you've overcome together?

....

....

....

....

....

....

....

....

....

....

....

....

Losing friends sucks, but sometimes we grow apart from our besties. It's just one of those things that happens from time to time.
Is there someone in your life you're dying to hang out with again? What would you say if you had a chance to chat with them tomorrow?

Set goals. Whether they're big or small goals, to do with school, friends, family or what you want to achieve personally – it all starts with a plan.

With your goals in mind, seek out a mentor. This might be an awesome teacher, parent, neighbor, big sister, sports coach, a co-worker, boss or a friend.

Surround yourself with good people. Misery loves company and there's nothing more draining than being around toxic people. Get out – get to somewhere that makes YOU happy. Find your crew.

Don't apologize for having dreams, desires and thoughts of your own.

Learn from setbacks. Don't take them to heart – try to see the lesson in the madness and move forward smarter and stronger than ever.

People worth impressing:

1. You right now

2. Your 80-year-old self

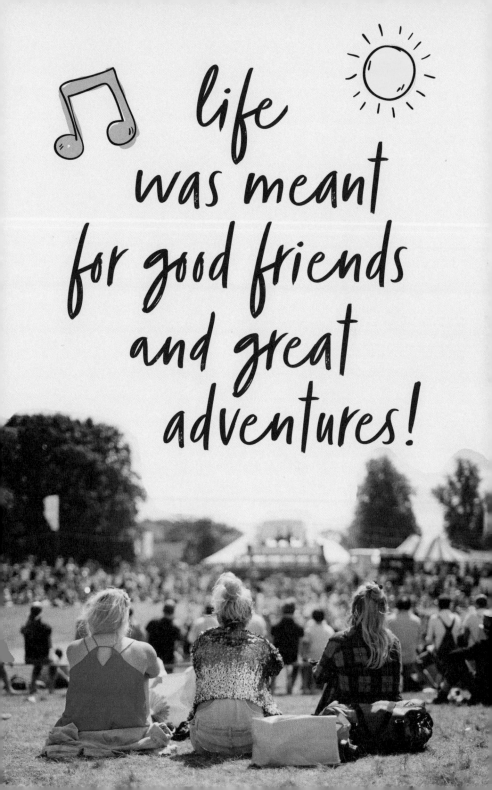

"Sisterhood is something so valid and important when you are growing up that I literally think the essence of it should be taught in schools, but the 'squads' we see in the media are very polarizing. Feminism and friendship are supposed to be inclusive, and most of these 'squads' are strictly exclusive."

Rowan Blanchard

Rowan Blanchard might be best known for her role on the hit series *Girl Meets World*, but it's her outspoken stance on feminism, queer issues and race issues that has the world falling in love with her over and over again.

TRUE FRIENDSHIP
ISN'T ABOUT
WHO CAME FIRST
OR WHO YOU'VE
KNOWN THE
LONGEST.
IT'S ABOUT WHO
CAME AND
NEVER LEFT.

"I believe that it is as much a right and duty for women to do something with their lives as for men and we are not going to be satisfied with such frivolous parts as you give us."

Louisa May Alcott

Louisa May Alcott wrote one of the most popular young adult novels of all time: *Little Women*. Besides being a kickass author, she was also a feminist and abolitionist.

When someone
asks what
I'm passionate
about ...

ME: Making the
world a safer
place for girls.

"There's something so special about a woman who dominates in a man's world. It takes a certain grace, strength, intelligence, fearlessness, and the nerve to never take no for an answer."

Rihanna

Who wouldn't stand under Rihanna's umbrella? The famous singer is an unapologetic feminist and even protested in front of Trump Tower during the New York City Women's March.

If you could have dinner with any five women
in the world, who would they be and why?
This is your fantasy female team! Think about
friends, family members, celebrities, politicians,
activists or women throughout history...

1

2

3

4

5

WOMEN TO WHOA ABOUT

Marjory Stoneman Douglas

Before the name 'Marjory Stoneman Douglas' became synonymous with the tragic school shooting at Marjory Stoneman Douglas High School in Parkland, Florida, on February 14, 2018, it was best known as the namesake of one of America's leading female authors, conservationists and women's suffrage advocates.

Marjory Stoneman Douglas was a force to be reckoned with. She lived to 108 years of age and was most famous for her work protecting the Florida Everglades, after they were threatened with being drained and reclaimed for major development.

When she passed away in 1998, London newspaper, *The Independent*, wrote a poignant obituary that stated, "In the history of the American environmental movement, there have been few more remarkable figures than Marjory Stoneman Douglas."

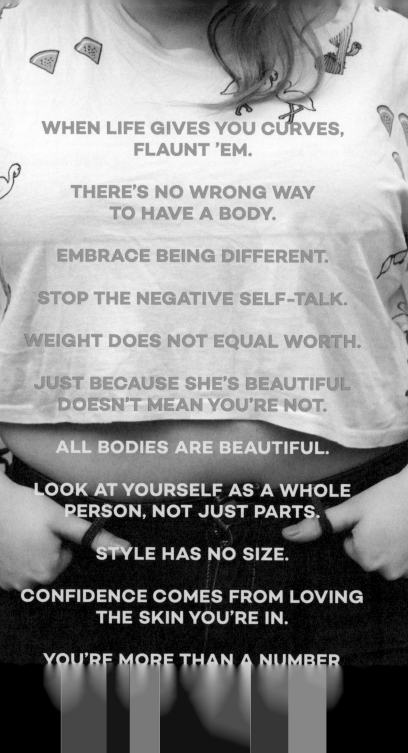

WHEN LIFE GIVES YOU CURVES,
FLAUNT 'EM.

THERE'S NO WRONG WAY
TO HAVE A BODY.

EMBRACE BEING DIFFERENT.

STOP THE NEGATIVE SELF-TALK.

WEIGHT DOES NOT EQUAL WORTH.

JUST BECAUSE SHE'S BEAUTIFUL
DOESN'T MEAN YOU'RE NOT.

ALL BODIES ARE BEAUTIFUL.

LOOK AT YOURSELF AS A WHOLE
PERSON, NOT JUST PARTS.

STYLE HAS NO SIZE.

CONFIDENCE COMES FROM LOVING
THE SKIN YOU'RE IN.

YOU'RE MORE THAN A NUMBER

Not everyone loves the gym. Not everyone wants abs. Not everyone makes friends with salad.

And that's OK.

Oh, unrealistic beauty standards — why you gotta be like that? In a world of filters and never-ending airbrushing, it often feels like we're in survival-of-the-prettiest mode all day, every day. Obsession with physical perfection is at an all-time high. Our self-esteem is low and we're self-hatin' like it's going out of fashion. But chasing the idea of flawless beauty and the perfect body isn't going to get us anywhere. That's not to say we should stop brushing our hair or putting on makeup if that's what we want, but let's do it because it makes us happy (props to you if that's already the case). Not just because we feel we should, or we're trying to look nice for someone else.

We're all unique. We need to start loving our curves, bumps, bony bits and changing figures because they're part of what makes us special. Sure, sometimes it can be hard to embrace our physical individuality. Especially when there's no shortage of people telling us what to wear, how to act, what to look like and how to feel about our bodies. The first step to turning that around is by being kinder to ourselves. Why? Because self-love and acceptance rules! It spreads all the good vibes. It's important to love what we've got, treat our bodies right and celebrate our physical differences. Love yourselves, and love each other.

"All bodies should be celebrated ... Beauty comes in all forms."

Gabi Gregg

Gabi Fresh, as she's best known, is a world-famous blogger and champion of plus-size girls and fashion. Gabi first started her blog when she finished university and couldn't land an entry-level fashion job. Now she has her own line of swimwear and hundreds of thousands of followers.

#justsayin

Have you ever wondered why girls are expected to pluck, shave, color, primp and prod every part of themselves but boys can get away with just having a shower? All this does is fuel insecurity and cause girls to spend money on products they don't need while also spending countless hours in front of the mirror. But the beauty industry loves it when we judge ourselves based on our looks.

If all girls woke up tomorrow morning and decided they were happy just as they are, think of how many industries would go out of business.

IN A SOCIETY THAT PROFITS FROM YOUR INSECURITIES, LOVING YOURSELF IS AN ACT OF REBELLION.

WE COME IN ALL
SHAPES AND SIZES,
AND ALL SKIN TONES.
WE HAVE FRECKLES,
STRETCH MARKS,
MOLES, DIMPLES,
BEAUTY SPOTS, LIGHT
HAIR, DARK HAIR –
NO HAIR AT ALL. AND
THAT'S GREAT. IT'S
THE BEAUTY OF BEING
A GIRL – OF BEING
UNIQUE AND AN
INDIVIDUAL.

"Don't put me in a box because I have dreads and tattoos or assume I'm a hippie. I'm not obligated to be anybody's anything. I'm a human. I will make mistakes. I will change my mind. I will figure things out as I go. I want people to see something authentic and real and achievable. You don't have to become a movie star. And you don't have to straighten your hair. You don't have to be the girlfriend or the side chick or the cute one or the sexy one. You can be just whoever you are, and people are going to see that and they're going to love it. And that's how you're going to succeed in life, mentally and physically."

Sasha Lane

As a psychology and social work major, Sasha's life took an unexpected turn when she was talent-spotted at a beach and later cast in an award-winning film. Since then she's spoken openly about mental health, feminism and body image issues.

YOU: Makeup is false advertising

ME: Oh that's funny, because I'm not a product – and I'm not trying to sell myself to you.

aviolafyre.tumblr.com

When do you feel your best?

DIET TIPS

1. Write a list of all the people in your life who have a problem with your weight.

2. Cut them out of your life.

3. Feel lighter instantly.

"My great hope for us as young women is to start being kinder to ourselves so that we can be kinder to each other. To stop shaming ourselves and other people ... too fat, too skinny, too short, too tall, too anything. There's a sense that we're all 'too' something, and we're all not enough."

Emma Stone

Emma Stone might be an Academy Award–winning actress but it's her role as the super smart and independent teen Olive Penderghast in *Easy A* that will always be our favorite. Cool fact? When Emma was accepting her Oscar for *La La Land*, she was wearing a Planned Parenthood pin on her dress in support of the non-profit women's reproductive health organization.

There's no right or wrong way to be a girl.

Just because you love fashion, style and beauty doesn't mean you don't have the right to comment on politics, culture and society.

"I don't do anything technically brave. I just sit here, discuss my insecurities and get better at loving myself. It seems pretty simple, right? I guess it's not. See, we've made our bodies an unsafe place to exist ... That is why, when I sit crossed-legged showing you a body that is underrepresented in our media, I get hailed as doing an act of bravery."

Kenzie Brenna

Kenzie Brenna is an actress, YouTube star and body positive activist.

HOW TO DRESS LIKE A GIRL

Be a girl.

Put on literally any piece of clothing.

Congratulations – you are now dressed like a girl!

IT'S NOT THE SIZE OF THE GIRL IN THE FIGHT, IT'S THE SIZE OF THE FIGHT IN THE GIRL!

"**Spend less time tearing yourself apart wondering if you're good enough. You are good enough.**"

Reese Witherspoon

Elle Woods in *Legally Blonde* reminded us all that girls can do anything — even if they're underestimated by their family, friends and boyfriends! No one could have played that role quite like Reese.

Thick is cute

Skinny is cute

Fat is cute

ALL BODIES
ARE CUTE *

"One of the most important things I've learned in my life is the importance of loving yourself. When I do motivational speeches or even tell myself 'Love yourself' (and you should love yourself), I'm aware it comes across very cliché. I tell myself, 'Okay, I sound like a Tumblr quote.' But really, if you actually think about it, a lot of us don't love ourselves."

Lilly Singh

What a bawse! Not only is Lilly a famous YouTube personality, vlogger and writer, she's also a hilarious comedian and actress. You might know this Canadian talent by her online name: IISuperwomanII

Which words and phrases do you and your
friends use to describe your bodies?

Circle the positive words and draw a line
through the negative ones.
How many did you have of each?

I AM WHOLE AS I AM

WOMEN TO WHOA ABOUT

Michelle Payne

It might have been 155 years in the making, but in 2015 Michelle Payne became the first female jockey to win the Melbourne Cup horse race. Michelle was only the fourth female jockey to ever ride in the Cup. "It's a very male-dominated sport," she has said, "and people think we are not strong enough ... I'm so glad to the win Melbourne Cup and, hopefully, it will help female jockeys from now on to get more of a go."

He For She

As part of the ongoing fight for women's equality, it only makes sense that we want all boys and men to identify as feminists too. But there's a fine line between tokenistic feminism and actually believing in and fighting for the rights of women. We need to ensure we don't have boys and men trying to save us from the patriarchy by becoming knights in shining armor. What we need is for them to stand by our side and support us – just like we do for them, and just like we should all do for each other. We don't need men to be champions of women – rather, we should be champions for all other human beings, regardless of gender, age, size, sex, color or privilege. By creating a solid foundation of feminism among boys and girls, and teaching men to respect women, we're working towards a society that finally treats everyone as an equal.

66

What feminism means to me is that you don't let your gender define who you are — you can be who you want to be, whether you're a man, a woman, a boy, a girl, whatever.

—Joseph Gordon-Levitt

99

DON'T BE THAT GUY

It's important that we remind the boys and men in our life that it's not good enough to just SAY they support women's rights, but then still expect women to cook, clean and look after them because it's "the way it's always been." When a girl gets angry, it's not an opportunity for boys to make a joke about hormones or periods. When a girl has an opinion, it's not OK for boys to call her names. And when a girl has a problem, it's not up to the boy to solve it. We don't need to be saved. We can do that ourselves.

WHAT'S A BOY TO DO?

Well, there are a few things actually.
Here are some tips you can give to boys
in your life.

If we have a problem, listen.

Don't give us advice unless we ask for it.

Don't judge us.

Talk to your friends about the way they talk
about or to women.
Are they being sexist?
Chat it out and educate.

Don't undervalue our problems and don't pretend
to be able to relate to problems you'll never
experience or understand.

Use your privilege for good: point out
sexist behavior when you see it.

Lead by example.

People of
quality
aren't scared
of equality

BOY
OH
BOY
DO
GIRLS
RULE

He offered her
the world and
she said she had
her own.

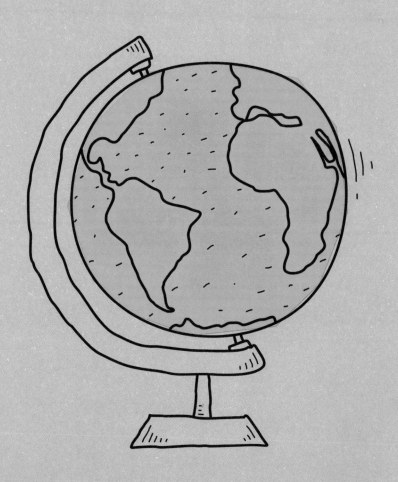

AND THEN THERE WAS YOU

Look at that! You got to the end of the book. Hopefully you're feeling more empowered than ever to champion real change out there in the big, wide world. There's no sugar-coating the fact that the road ahead is hard. Like… really hard. But we have to take on the challenge to achieve equality and finally acknowledge people as people, regardless of their color, sex or gender.

While there will be plenty of people who claim things are fine just the way they are, or that we've already done enough for women, it's important to remember that advancing gender equality is an ongoing battle.

Believe in yourself and the power you hold – because, girl, you're unstoppable.

"

The future belongs to those who believe in the beauty of their dreams.

—Eleanor Roosevelt

"

MY FEMINIST TIME CAPSULE:
Find an empty box at home and fill it
with all the things that remind you of the
awesomeness of being a girl. What is it that
inspires you? Fill the box with inspirational
quotes, pictures of your favorite women,
books that have made a difference to your
life and advice from your best friends. If you
can hold out, tuck the box away and don't
look at it for five years! Future you will love
you for it!

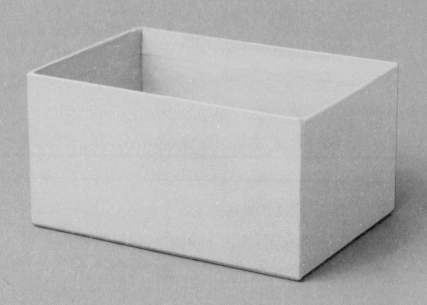

Fill this in and write from the heart. Make it count — it's the last message of the book.

TO: Me

FROM: Me

MESSAGE:

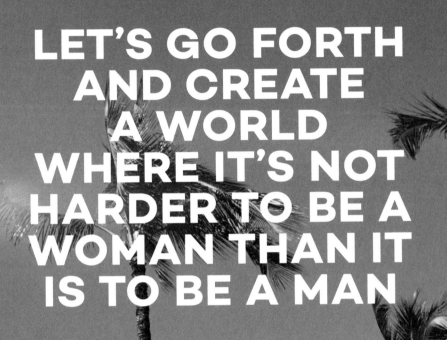

LET'S GO FORTH
AND CREATE
A WORLD
WHERE IT'S NOT
HARDER TO BE A
WOMAN THAN IT
IS TO BE A MAN

WHO CAN I TALK TO?

Whether you're going through a rough patch, have things you need to get off your chest, or you just wanna chat – there are a ton of amazing services that offer seriously awesome support and advice. What's best is that they're here for you whenever you need them. From mental health worries to physical health questions, strategies for dealing with bullies, school pressures, or problems at home – these guys are here to listen and lighten your load.

Here are some support services that are totally free, super helpful and completely confidential:

Teen Line, teenlineonline.org

YourLifeYourVoice.org

CrisisTextLine.org

TheBullyProject.com

Glossary

Cisgender: Someone whose gender identity aligns with the sex they were given at birth.

Feminism: The belief in and desire for equality between men and women.

Gender: The social and cultural state of being male or female.

Intersectionality: The way in which race, class, ethnicity, religion, sexual orientation and disability status are interconnected and affect the way individual people are discriminated against and oppressed.

LGBTQI: Lesbian, gay, bisexual, transgender, queer and intersex. Some people also use the Q to stand for "questioning".

Non-binary: Someone who doesn't identify as being female or male, a woman or a man.

Patriarchy: The system we all live under, whereby men are privileged and generally given power.

Privilege: When some people in society have advantages over others.

Sexism: The notion that women are inferior to men.

Transgender: Someone whose gender identity is different to the sex they were assigned at birth.

Women of color: Women who aren't white or of European heritage.

REMEMBER, YOUR VIBE ATTRACTS YOUR TRIBE